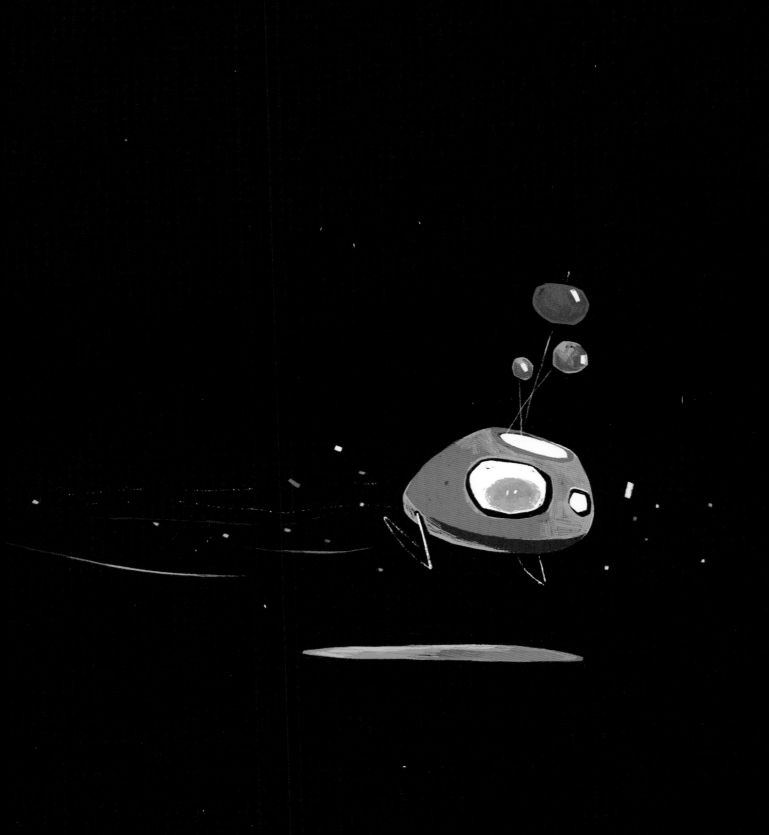

MARIO AND THE ALIENS

TEXT BY CAROLINA ZANOTTI
ILLUSTRATIONS BY TAMYPU

Happy Fox
BOOKS

Mario was playing on the computer in his room, as he usually did.

Suddenly, he heard a really loud noise in the yard.

When he ran outside, he couldn't see a thing.

But he could hear whistling, steaming, and beeping.

He pushed his glasses up on his nose and saw the flashing, whirling, colorful lights of a . . .

. . . 100% real spaceship in his backyard!

It was purple.

It was huge.

He couldn't see inside.

The windows were shiny as a mirror.

So Mario stepped closer and closer and closer until

. . . a window opened and out popped
a real, live space creature.

He was taller than Mario's dad.

He was round. He was green. And he was very, very furry.

The alien smiled, blinked his eyes twice, and waved hello with
all ten of his hands.

He reminded Mario of a fuzzy kiwi fruit.

The alien looked like he was about to say something, when . . .

. . . he was pushed out
of the way by another
alien who was much,
much taller than
Mario's dad.

The alien looked like a
cow and a banana,
all in one!

Wriggling behind
the cow/banana
alien was something
mysterious.

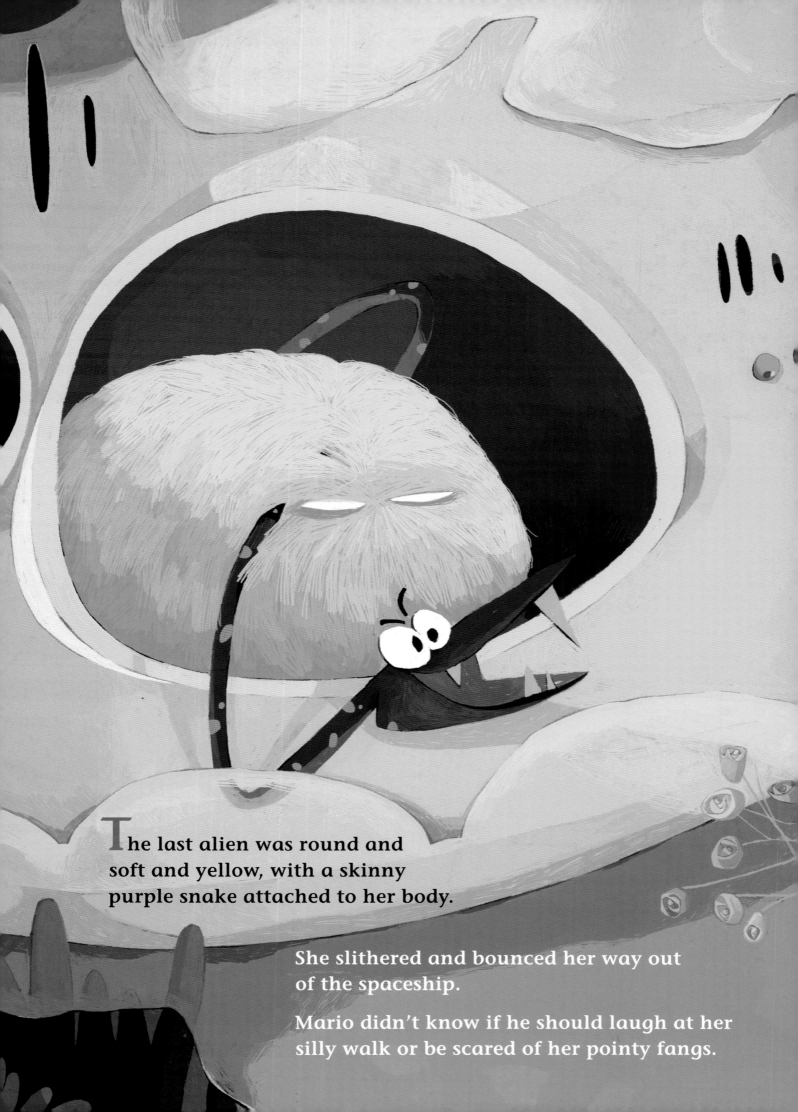

The last alien was round and soft and yellow, with a skinny purple snake attached to her body.

She slithered and bounced her way out of the spaceship.

Mario didn't know if he should laugh at her silly walk or be scared of her pointy fangs.

When Mario saw the three aliens looking at him, he really was scared.

He ran to get his mom and dad.

"Wait!" said the green one. "We just want to play. We're looking for some new friends and fun games.

We flew here from Boresix, the most boring planet
in the universe. My name is Decimus."

The snake smiled. "I am Missalien."

"Please call me Yorso," said the biggest alien

Mario went from being scared to being happy and excited.

"Three new alien friends!" he whispered to himself.

He told the aliens, "Please wait here. I'll be right back!"

Mario proudly brought
his computer outside
to his new friends.

Yorso rolled his eyes.
"Not more computers!" he complained.

Missalien hissed in disappointment.

"I thought you humans were different,"
Decimus sniffed. "Let's get back on the
spaceship. I guess we have to find a more
interesting planet."

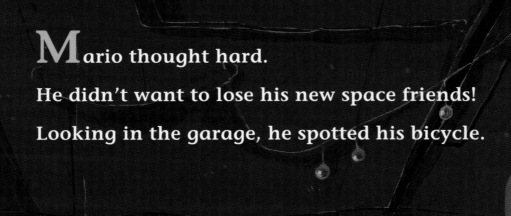

Mario thought hard.

He didn't want to lose his new space friends!

Looking in the garage, he spotted his bicycle.

"I bet you don't have bikes on your planet. I'll teach you to ride mine. Who wants to go first?"

"Me, me, me! I love riding bikes!" shouted Yorso. "Umm . . . which one is a bike?"

Mario helped Yorso up on the bike. His body was squishy and not very heavy.

Yorso fell off three times before he could peddle the bike.

Mario cheered, "You did it!"

Missalien and Decimus shouted, "Hooray! Now we can all ride together!"

"Mario first," said Yorso. So Mario climbed up and sat in Yorso's squishy lap.

Then Missalien bounced up high and wrapped herself around Yorso's neck.

Decimus held on with all ten hands.

They laughed as they rode around the yard.

But Yorso didn't know how to use bicycle brakes!

They all toppled over in a bouncy, furry, giggling pile on the grass.

"That was great!" said the aliens. "What's next?"

"**I** know just the thing!"
said Mario.

The aliens waited in the living room
while Mario ran upstairs.

He brought down one of his little
sister's dolls and beauty kit.

"Ooooh! That's so pretty,"
said Missalien.

Before Mario knew what
was happening . . .

... he had a pink bow in his hair and his face was covered with makeup!

Mario and his friends went to the basement next.

Mario picked up his soccer ball and announced, "My friends, let me introduce you to the greatest game in the world!"

Mario led the aliens out to the yard.

He explained the rules of soccer.

They took turns keeping goal
while the rest tried to score.

When no one could score against
Decimus, with his ten arms and
hands, they stopped.

They all collapsed on the ground,
tired and hot and happy.

"Wait here, I'll be right back,"
said Mario.

"This is so much fun," he thought,
as he brought out some drinks and
a few more toys.

Yorso's drink was still half full when he fell asleep, snoring loudly. Missalien was the next to fall asleep.

"This isn't good," thought Mario. "We have so many more games to play."

All of a sudden the spaceship started beeping.

Its lights were blinking a pattern: red, orange, green, red, orange, green.

Decimus woke up his friends. "We're going to be late! Our parents' reminder signal is flashing! It's time to go."

"Wait!" said Mario. "Take the toys with you so you can practice for next time. You'll come back, won't you?"

"Of course, Mario! This day was the most fun ever. Be sure to think of lots of new games for next time!" Yorso said.

As the spaceship flew away, Mario thought about how much fun he had playing with his friends.

Then he realized that he hadn't missed his computer at all!

Mario decided that tomorrow he would ask his parents to take him to the playground.

He had more new friends to make.

Thai My Phuong, aka **Tamypu**, was born and raised in Da Nang City, Vietnam, and studied interior design in Saigon. She also earned a master's degree in sequential design and illustration in the UK.

Carolina Zanotti is a journalist specializing in music and theater. She has written several successful stories and theater shows for children.

Conversation Starters for Parents

The amount of time young children spend in front of a screen is an issue worldwide. Ask your child some questions about this story to get them thinking about ways to have fun away from a screen.

1 What games would you have taught the aliens?

2 Which of your toys would you have shared?

3 What games do you think Mario will teach the aliens when they visit again?

4 Why don't the aliens want to play computer games?

5 Which alien would you want to be? Why?

Happy Fox Books is an imprint of Fox Chapel Publishing Company, Inc., 903 Square Street, Mount Joy, PA 17552.

© 2019 Snake SA, Chemin du Tsan du Péri 10, 3971 Chermignon, Switzerland

Mario and the Aliens is an original work, first published in North America in 2019 by Fox Chapel Publishing Company, Inc. Reproduction of its contents is strictly prohibited without written permission from the rights holder.

ISBN 978-1-64124-040-6 (paperback)
ISBN 978-1-64124-027-7 (hardcover)

The Cataloging-in-Publication data is on file with the Library of Congress.

To learn more about the other great books from Fox Chapel Publishing,
or to find a retailer near you, call toll-free 800-457-9112 or visit us at
www.FoxChapelPublishing.com.

We are always looking for talented authors. To submit an idea, please send a brief inquiry to
acquisitions@foxchapelpublishing.com.

Fox Chapel Publishing makes every effort to use environmentally friendly paper for printing.

Printed in China